Playground Science

CITY SCIENCE

Thomas F. Sheehan

www.rourkeeducationalmedia.com

© 2006 Rourke Educational Media

All rights reserved. No part of this book may be reproduced or utilized in any form or by any means, electronic or mechanical including photocopying, recording, or by any information storage and retrieval system without permission in writing from the publisher.

www.rourkeeducationalmedia.com

PHOTO CREDITS: Cover © Getty images; title page © Ivan Philipou; page 4 © Painet, Inc.; pages 6, 12 © Photodisc; page 9 © Timothy Vacula; pages 15, 16, 17, 18, 20, 22, 23 © P.I.R.; page 21 © Image 100 LTD

Consulting editor: Marcia S. Freeman

Library of Congress Cataloging-in-Publication Data

Sheehan, Thomas F.
  Playground science / Thomas F. Sheehan.
    p. cm. -- (City science)
  Includes bibliographical references and index.
  ISBN 978-1-59515-410-1 (hardcover - English)
  ISBN 978-1-62717-235-6 (softcover - English)
  ISBN 978-1-60694-061-7 (e-Book - English)
  ISBN 978-1-62717-241-7 (softcover - Spanish)
  ISBN 978-1-62717-437-4 (e-Book - Spanish)

Printed in China, FOFO I - Production Company
  Shenzhen, Guangdong Province

rourkeeducationalmedia.com

customerservice@rourkeeducationalmedia.com • PO Box 643328 Vero Beach, Florida 32964

Table of Contents

Playground Science	5
Motion and Energy	7
Balance	10
Friction	13
Elastic Motion	16
Swinging Motion	19
Rotary Motion	20
Ramps and Stairs	22
Glossary	24
Index	24

Playground Science

City playgrounds have lots of fun equipment to play on. But did you know that your neighborhood or school playground is also a good place to learn about science? You can learn about motion and **energy**. You can learn about movement and balance.

Motion and Energy

You can move in all sorts of ways in a playground. You can push and pull, and you can go up and down. You can slide and glide, you can swing and spin. All this movement takes energy.

Climbing takes energy.

A tug of war takes a lot of **effort**. Everyone on the team uses energy to pull together. The team that uses the most energy usually wins!

Balance

An unbalanced seesaw

You probably know it is hard to balance a seesaw if one person is heavier than the other. The heavier person goes down with a bump! Sometimes the lighter person will go flying off the other end unless he or she hangs on tight!

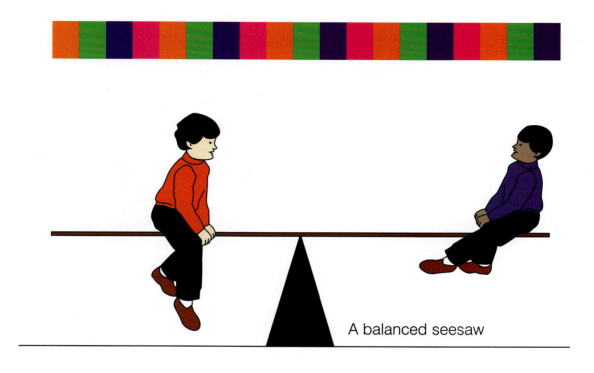

A balanced seesaw

But if the heavier person moves closer to the middle of the seesaw, that person can balance the seesaw. Balance depends on both your weight and how far you are from the middle of the seesaw. Try this with a friend.

Friction

A slippery slide gives you a fast ride. You go fast because there is not much friction between your clothes and the slide.

If you want to slow down, you can add more friction. Just press your shoes against the sides of the slide. Friction is the sticky force that slows you down when your shoes or skin rub the surface of the slide.

Friction helps you to hang by your hands. Your skin is sticky compared to the pipe. What might happen if you tried to hang by your hands in woolly mittens?

Elastic Motion

Does your playground have springy things to ride or bounce on? Springs are long pieces of wire wound in a tube shape. When you bend a spring, it bounces back to its original shape. Your weight and motion store energy in the spring as it bends. The energy makes the springs bounce back again. Boing! Back and forth you go!

When you jump on a trampoline, the springs store up your energy. When the stretched springs bounce back, you are tossed back up into the air.

Swinging Motion

It takes energy to enjoy the swings. You use energy when you "pump" the swing with your legs and body. The swing goes higher and higher.

Then, **gravity** pulls you back down. You go faster and faster. Then up you go the other way.

Your speed increases as you go down and decreases as you go up again. On the way down, doesn't it feel funny as you accelerate?

Rotary Motion

When you're on a spinning playground ride, you are rotating. Rotation means going around and around in one spot. Tops and pinwheels spin. They have rotary motion. Spinning can make you dizzy.

The wheels on your roller-blade skates rotate. You can go fairly fast on a smooth surface. There is little friction between your wheels and the surface.

Elbow pads and kneepads prevent friction from scraping your skin off. Is your school or neighborhood playground a good place to skate?

Wearing a helmet is a smart move.

Ramps and Stairs

Ramps lead you up or down from one level to another. Stairs, like ramps, take you up or down easily and safely. Stairs and ramps are **inclined** walkways.

Ramps and stairs can turn a big jump into a few easy steps. But sometimes it is more fun to jump and maybe take a lump!

Glossary

effort (EF urt) — use of energy to do something
energy (EN ur jee) — any force or power that can do something
gravity (GRAV ut ee) — a pulling force from the earth
inclined (IN KLYND) — slanted surfaces

Index

balance   10, 11
ramps   22
rotation   20
swings   19
trampoline   17

Further Reading

Madgwick, Wendy. On the Move. Raintree Steck-Vaughn, 2000
Welsbachre, Ann. Levers. Capstone 2000
Whitehouse, Patty. Friction. Rourke Publishing, 2004

About The Author

Thomas Sheehan lives, breathes, and teaches science in Maine. He credits the English Departments at Cornell University and SUNY for awakening his interest in good writing, E. B. White's Elements of Style for smoothing out the wrinkles, and the editors at The Bangor Daily News for discipline.